Lindokuhle
-Advantageous Mutation

By Brendon Mokalapa

About the book...

This is a short novel composed of about 5 chapters. In this book, the writer wrote a bit about his life (Love life) that even the name of the main character is his (Brendon). This book was inspired by a girl known as Lindokuhle. As Brendon is a different boy, like any other boy, the way he lives and the way he reacts, he thought this it is a bad difference, yet, without noticing, it was an advantageous difference. That is why he titled the book: Lindokuhle: The advantageous mutation. Mutation is a scientific term meaning that some genes processes have gone through mistakes as they were dividing to help us grow. Here are how the chapters are carried:

Table of Contents

Chapter 1:

Brendon, a matriculant, is in school most of the time and likes to be remaining behind for practicing maths. He then makes many promises to his future love life planning.

Chapter 2:

Brendon meets few challenges in his love life, he even thinks about previous relationship with Patience. He goes for a camp and meet a promise breaking girl. Coming back from the camp, he must recover first since it was tough. He hears about the dearth of his beloved uncle and at same he is heavily surprised by a stranger on one of the social media. This calls for his wisdom.

Chapter 3:

Brendon knows the stranger and its motive as he was worried. He then decides on what to do with the stranger, he chooses to allow her in.

Chapter 4:

It is exam time, so Brendon gives it a break. This

break breaks the stranger's heart. Brendon writes his final exams.

Chapter 5:

How life have been after Brendon finished with his exams. Then Brendon starts writing books. He becomes a writer of novels; he writes a book about his lady-friend.

About the author...

Brendon Mokalapa was a young man when he wrote this book, he was finishing his grade 12 in 2017. At around 4 he then moved to Ngwalemong, a village at the Rakgoadi region ruled by Queen Mokgoma. He attended school there until 2011 when he moved back to Tembisa, to Mashemong section, to complete his Primary School at Mashemong Primary school. He attended high school at Boitumelong secondary school. His first short story written but unfortunately lost was Mahlaelela (Meaning the one who always invites people when eating). Brendon Mokalapa is quite serious when busy, he is just unique, but not an outlier. He has a younger brother, younger sister and many cousins, as he is the first born. He was a young Preacher when he was writing this book. He wrote books like; Danny's Life sentence, The Devil in a fleshly coat; The family curse, Lengana and many more with poems.

Special thanks to...

First GOD Almighty for His Love, Will, Grace and Mercy. Then thanks to all supporting me(Brendon Mokalapa) by reading my books. Even though my parents never understood my writing desire, I thank them for the little friction they gave to my passion, instead of breaking me, it built and highly accelerated my action toward fulfilling my dream of getting published and satisfying my desire of writing. Another dream I would like to be fulfilled is that my writing be read also in schools. I than all my teachers, especially the one who was very close, supporting my writing, Ma'am Morukhu. Thanks, to all of you.

Chapter 1:

"Mutation is failure or a mistake that happens in the genes during cell division, and there are two types: an advantageous mutation and a disadvantageous mutation. Advantageous mutation is when the mistake in the genes happen for a good purpose, just like white moth in a dark environment. The moth which will have black colour because of mutation will be well structured for a dark environment. Mutation happens every time, that is why we vary in terms of genetic characteristics. Are we on the same page grade twelves?" Mr B shouting as they failed the previous test. "I am not a Life Sciences teacher for fun, and I did not just wake up one day and became a teacher. I worked very hard, so you work harder also. After last week's test I saw that my teaching was in vain. You see me shouting now, yet some will write rubbish. My period is over now, please get going to your next class". He shouts even more. "No sir, to remind you; it is double period. We are still attending here until we go for lunch." Brendon talks with a low voice. Then Mr B stands up again and continues with the shouting as he believes that learners hear more when a teacher shout." Now we proceed with genetics. I was still on mutation…"

It is lunch time now and Mariah is gossiping with her friends. "OH, if I could just date Joseph my life could be lived to the fullest, *wena* (Meaning you in Sotho) Julia, who is your current crush? Or you love everyone?" Mariah is talking while staring at Joseph. "No, I want to be like Brendon…" Julia sees Brendon approaching. "What is the talk about my name in this territory? What's the syllabus of this conclave?" Brendon asks. "No, we…we…we were…" Julia is caught off guard. "No, we were just talking about boyfriends and girlfriends" Matilda replies with confidence. "Then how did Coulomb's law apply here, as my name was mentioned?" Brendon added. "No! We were trying to think about your current girlfriend. You are a human being also Brendon and you do have feeling and have a crush on someone. Tell us who your crush is." Mariah manipulating words around. "Your just solving simultaneous equation with three unknowns, I do not have a girlfriend". Brendon adds. "But you love someone isn't it? Remember God is listening to us, and you are our pastor, you cannot lie to us." Mariah works out words. "I don't trust anyone, especially girls. All girls are parasitic and some even pathogenic. I hope to have no girlfriend for the rest of my life. I do lust for some, but I am different, I will not approach a lady, I have self-control. And besides, who likes someone like me?" Brendon justifies himself. "Let me go an eat, you remain here trying to solve Bloom's level four questions without a calculator". He then leaves them with their lower jaws few centimetres away from the ground.

When everyone heads home, Brendon is still few hours behind. At school flipping few pages of any science book he comes across. He is an addict of science yet a Christian. It is amazing how he manages two different worlds, especially when it comes to evolution in Life Sciences. Yet, as he said it during lunch, that he is different. Just like any other breathing being around the world, they vary in something. Yet again, as for Brendon, the variance from other people seems to be humongous. When it is time for Brendon to go home, he locks the class and when he is about to go out the school gate. He sees a lady with her face down. "Hey! What's wrong?" Brendon asks. "Nothing, just that I remember my former best friends. I am too lonely nowadays". Julia responds with her face still down as if she had been crying. "Nature selects its best sometimes. Worry not, mina (Meaning myself/I) I made God my Friend, just like Abraham did". Brendon tries to calm her down. "But I need a friend like you Brendon, one which can help me in class and spiritually. I need you Brendon please." Julia looks at Brendon eye to eye. "I am just a person of flesh and blood; one day they will fade away. Yet to promise you, The Word of God never passes away. Need God not me, for when trouble comes, I seek God also. He never sleeps, yet I sleep…" Brendon preaches." No! You do not understand me, Brendon. I mean I love…" Julia then cuts her words. "What?" Surprisingly. "No, never mind". She leaves Brendon running. "This lady has problems. She cannot just speak rhetoric staff and leave. What is her motive? She wants to be with me. No, I will have to ignore her by Scriptures. This is the only way. I cannot break my self-promises." Brendon speaks alone at the scene. Julia and Brendon never saw each other that day again, until tomorrow. When they met, Brendon started quoting Scriptures, and Julia tried to change the subject, but failed as Brendon is quite talkative when it comes to Scriptures. As they say, you only swim well where you know the corners and secretes of the pool.

At the school, just before lunch. Julia overhears voices talking about the boy of her dreams. "But I think that Brendon has a problem at home". "No! He is fine, I know how he lives at home. The problem I suspect is on gene flow". "You mean there might be a gene mutation somewhere?" Yes! There is no other explanation for his difference among our children. Perhaps a gene for feelings is mutated". "Mm! Yet that could be good for me. I tend to think that if it is mutation, then it is advantageous mutation. I just fought with my husband yesterday. It was to be better if I lived alone." "Your husband is just another man, yet he is better than mine. He just came home from the shebeen and slept on the sofa until I woke him up at midnight. Being single could…" Now Julia moves from her perfect position of hearing the gossip of two people at the class through the window. She then sees Brendon approaching and goes back a bit. "Now what am I going to do to draw his attention? Maybe I should just read one scripture, memorise it and go and sing it before him". She quickly opens a small old, covered Bible and reads. "Hey Brendon! How are you doing today man of God?" She asks "Since when do you call me man of God. On what side of the bed did you wake up on today? Yet I know that to all there is a season, a time for every purpose under Heaven." Brendon smiles.

"And without controversy. Great is the Mystery of godliness: God was manifested in flesh, justified in Spirit, seen by Angels." Julia does as she planned. "Preached among the Gentiles, believed on in the world, received up in glory. Wow, that is 1 Timothy 3 verse 16. When did you read it?" He is surprised." Yesterday. I was reading and this one touched me. Can you explain it to me please?" Julia adds. "Ok! But if you do not get me, it is ok. It takes The Holy Spirit to reveal it unto you to see it". Brendon responds quicker. The two now sit together, Brendon explaining Scriptures while Julia's attention is fully on Brendon's face. She is just saying "yes" nonstop, just to draw more of Brendon's attention. She even gets closer to Brendon that she might even touch him a little, to just try to make him feel somehow. But Brendon is in spirit, quoting verses continuously.

Chapter 2:

High-flyer's camp is set forth for all matriculants, and they are preparing for this five-day camp. It is the first camp of this kind ever in the district Brendon schools at. Brendon heard some of his classmates yesterday talking about girls, that they are going to get many girlfriends.

So, this rang a bell in Brendon's love life. He remembered Patience, who was his first girlfriend. Yet she did not consider herself as a girlfriend as she was over hundred kilometres away from this unique young boy. Patience dated with Brendon in a long distant relationship, and she was sucking him financially.

They dated for a year and few months, ever since a cousin to Patience, whom was an almost friend but a church mate to Brendon induced the relationship by distributing number phones. Brendon called off the relationship after discovering that Patience is dating others besides him. Brendon was quite naughty when it comes to technology because he managed to reveal former Patience's boyfriend on internet. How investigative is that? This matter made Patience live in fear, and when she started dating near herself, short distance relationships, she let Brendon know before he could know about it. These two only met twice face to face in that year of relationship. And they only touched each other once (Not a hug, nor a kiss, but just a few seconds touch). That is one of the reasons why Brendon said that he never dated a girl to that date.

Now Brendon proceeds preparing for five-day camp. He is just thinking a little about what he needs to wear. So as the day of departure arrived, he was ready. They left and arrived at a certain place, called Tieger lodge. The first hour they arrived there they start revising with teachers from other schools. I will not say much in this matter, because even when I was there with them, I noticed how Brendon had been for that five-days.

So, allow me to just tell you the way Brendon reacted towards girls. Do not ask me how I knew his feelings. Brendon was just starring and scanning new faces ever in his life, and some faces were similar. On the third day, he saw a girl in an accounting class. She was sited co-linear to Brendon and the white board where Brendon was looking. All his attention was swept away from class to that girl. The girl was very beautiful. In Brendon's mind was never a thought that he does not desire a girl. This one changed everything in his life (Promises).

Then Brendon prayed a bit as the lesson was coming to an end and asked God to deliver that lady before him according to His Will. The Lord, The Provider provided. Late around nine in the evening as Brendon and classmates from school were practicing maths, here came that pretty girl. With no pimple, black spot nor any mistake on her body. I am sure she had a millennium of boyfriends.

The way she was so pretty, no boy could let her pass. She just came and sat few metres away from Brendon. Just as it happened at the accounting class, it also happened here; All His attention was swept away from the lesson. Now in his heart was Ecclesiastes 3; To all there is a season, a time for every purpose under Heaven.

So, he started realising that his mouth is not well. This is not an everyday thing; it is just mostly for the 12 hours learning without saying serious words. So, the mouth is really pressurised. Then he started asking her questions while looking the other way. As he spoke, one of his classmates called the name of this pretty girl. "Sane", a name first time heard by Brendon's ears. Then it was all coming alright until two boys came from nowhere and called Sane (The pretty girl).

Then Brendon's heart started becoming somehow, then he then became speechless. He then tried to concentrate on maths but could not. Moreover, because the two boys just sat with the pretty girl just few metres away from Brendon, and they seem to be discussing Geography, which is a foreign language to Brendon that he may interfere. Brendon just went to sleep without saying bye to his classmates.

From that time, he saw Sane again the hour when buses arrived, leaving the camp for home. He could only look at her this time since there were many people around them chatting, and not only that, but he is also a lay pastor, so this might mislead his people (Learners listening to him when preaching).

The whole month, Brendon was not himself after the dream of that girl. I say it is a dream because he did not touch, or able to repeat what happened. He does not know where that girl schools, the only thing he can do is just to remember how she looks, that if they meet in the future by God's Grace he might try again. A life of a preacher is very difficult, especially when still a teenager.

For all the teenage life changes, he will try to avoid. Just like dating. What makes it more tough is that people despise the preacher dating, yet they like him having a family. Is that possible? It is just as bad as how people hate a pregnant woman, but they love children a lot. How can there be a child without pregnancy? Unless that child is just a non-breathing creature.

I love a pure life a lot, yet how can one live pure without realising their mistakes? And how can a person know his mistake if he did not do it? How can you make a mistake if you tried nothing? You will have to do something if it is wrong you leave it. That is how pure life should be. Not stealing, seeing that it is bad, yet proceeding the madness. Just imagine; how would it be if everyone were the same? It was going to be perfect.

If all we steal, we steal all from all, and that will not be wrong before us. If all we care, we care for all at all, and that will not be a problem to anyone. If all we were mentally disturbed, no one would realise that we are mentally disturbed. Life could be better that way. That is one of the reasons educations is forced on all children, that we be equal and the same. Without wealth and poverty, how would it be? Nice, isn't it?

Enough about what I think friend, just read further as a write further about how Brendon lived trying to recover from that dream of that pretty girl. I really feel pity sometimes, for that poor Brendon. He is one of a kind in need and in deed. He cannot change easily since he is already having a plant of Scripture in him. For him to change, one must take him to the bush for ages, that he might forget even the quadratic formula.

I feel sorry for him since many people are not spiritually ok. They really hate him. Mostly those living close to him. For most parents compare his behaviour with their children's behaviour before their children. This is bad. He is even wise that he trusts no one, and he Thank God for that Wisdom of no trusting anyone.

One of the days he was just sitting, and as he was sitting like that (In class), he received a call from the mother. She let him know that his uncle is no longer his uncle, but the late uncle. His heart received a great shock, but he remembered many Scriptures like 1 Corinthian 15.

That even dearth is one of us, before we leave the world and pass it (Dearth). As he was to prepare for that, here is a conversation which took place on one of the social media:" Hey, is this Brendon?" A stranger asks." Yes, and you are?" Brendon replies and questions." Just forget about that. I want to tell you something".

"Ok! But tell me your name first". "Brendon! I am ashamed to say this, but since last year when you were in grade 11, I just looked at you. And every time I saw you, I just felt somehow. I always smile when I see you. I love you, Brendon. I cannot hold it. I have held it for a year now, and I know how bad it is for a lady to approach a boy. I hate myself for this, but I will feel better since I told you. Please forgive me for telling this to you neh".

The stranger said. "What is this now? Who is this now? How come? No, I cannot accept this. It is a trap! Most people hate me, even teachers. This is one of their fruits". Brendon thinks in his heart now, then he types; "If you tell me who you are first, perhaps you could win a check pot. Please tell me. Or you want me to investigate you?" Brendon asks. "Yes, go ahead please, just know that I am in grade 11".

From this now, Brendon was thinking. Then he said in his heart that he will wait for grade 11s to gather, then he will call the number of the lady or even a boy who is used in this trap. He was just having an intrapersonal conflict. The collision of ideas just flew in his brain and heart. Then he had to prepare to go and bury his beloved uncle. This was as if it's a curse or something.

All are strangers as he arrives, but he realises few faces even as he forgot their names. No one seems to be knowing him or caring that Brendon is around. He just gave all the respected elder visitors space to lay down at the house. And he slept that night at the independent friend's car. It was not a friend, it was a church mate, having a very long robe to connect the family.

At the morning Brendon wears a suit after taking a bath with elder men. As he is quite respected for living in the urban areas, he then sits down at the memorial service of his late uncle. He is requested to say few words on behalf of niece. But his mother warned him first to not preach, for an elder preacher was still coming to preach.

The programme director directs the service well, and calls Brendon. He stands, goes forth and wait for the haem to end so he can speak. "Greetings elders! I am so young to stand before you, yet I thank all of you for bringing support to bury my uncle. As his niece, and again representing all other niece. I say that we will always remember him.

He was loving children a lot, and always teasing them to grow tougher yet stronger. I loved him like all my uncles. I remember Ecclesiastes 3 from verse 1 which say, to all there is a season, a time for every purpose under heaven. A time to be born and a time to die. A time to plant and a time to pluck what is planted. I again thank you all for coming and thank you. Back to you programme director, let me not cause much friction to this service".

Brendon spoke as much as he planned, and he felt well after speaking. The memorial service ended, and cars were filled as they were escorting the late uncle to his last journey.

Chapter 3:

It is about a week since the burial of Brendon's uncle, and he only discovered that that stranger is either a Zulu or a Xhosa since he tried to catch her by speaking his own language. Now the stranger felt somehow and said this:

"I am Lindokuhle." Said the stranger on one of the social media networks. "Lindokuhle from where? I do not know you. Please send me your picture" There was no proper thinking in Brendon's mind as he is saying these words. He was still stressed from his uncle's passing. The girl, who claims to be Lindokuhle sent the picture. To Brendon's eyes the girl was beautiful and quiet.

She is not that much talkative like all girls he suspected to be doing that. He was even surprised if this can be the girl doing this brave stuff. He then said this after thinking of the consequences: "Let us meet. Where do you live?". "Not so far from where you stay", the stranger said. So, this became an arranged meeting as Brendon wanted to ensure that this lady is true.

Not a scam. So, he went to meet her, then to his surprise, this lady is true. She was a bit shy, wearing a brown trouser and a white shirt. Walking with two friend I think, and the friends left. So, they met and started speaking awkward words only.

As Brendon wanted to go to school, he asked the lady to escort him to school, but she was too shy. So, she went with him few metres and they hugged and repelled. This was so surprising to both parties. You approach a boy and he agree, and on the other side a girl approach you and you just let her in so easily.

Then later they spoke on the social network: "Please tell me this; What did you see in me that you like me?" Brendon asks. "Your just different, you're not like any other boy. You seem very smart, unique, and I like you the way you are. I love you, Brendon."

Replied the stranger named Lindokuhle. So, in Brendon's mind was the answer which always troubled him. At why he is so different and is there anyone who likes him for his variance. He then saw that his gene mutation was good and advantageous as it even attracts girls. Lindokuhle is not the first one to do this. Even some of her classmates tried this in a different way but Brendon could not let them in. He let her in because he was not hundred percent himself.

Remember that he promised himself, so from his uncle's dearth, he was no longer himself, that even greatest promises he promised could be broken. But he felt happy and forgetting about his late uncle and the loss of that dream girl. So, this Lindokuhle became a healing medicine to him, that he even somehow though she was sent by God Almighty. They then dated secretly. But as Lindokuhle loved him more that he did, she even told her elder brother and sister about this unique guy.

What Brendon went through here makes me crave for his mutation if truly there is such. He is attracting girls, and they fall on him like rain, that like a fisherman he chooses the best fish. If I were him, I would easily accept all, but that is trouble because it will cover his variance. Because Brendon's variance is that he is never seen dating a girl or approaching a lady. He is always busy and walking fast. When he dates, he dates only one lady and reject others, no matter how beautiful they can be.

Just think about that, who can do that? If I were in his shoes, I would have had a Moriah of girlfriends. If girls come to you without you approaching them, then once you start moving towards them, they will be just saying 'yes' 'yes'. But there is something I learned about life. I think Brendon is just ok the way he is this is advantageous mutation from other players (Boys who love girls).

What I learned about life is that what is mostly wanted, when found it is even despised. So, if you get many girls, many will start to repel from you as girls hate sharing. Look at a simple thing for example, a chew gum. A chew gum is well wanted by many, but one or two chew it, no one wants it. Do you want to be like a chewed gum? So, try to date one girl. Airtime paper for another practical example.

Many people want that airtime paper, and until one buy it and takes what attracted him (The voucher), he will through it far away and forget about it. From that time no one will want to see it. It will only be those people collecting rubbish or those recycling that they will just pick it up thinking money in their brains. So be like Brendon if you can unless his behaviour is genetically inspired.

I would highly be high with joy if I one day woke up and saw that I am Brendon. He is hated by many, but the once who hate him are losers. His lovers are perfect, beautiful, handsome and some genetically mutated if that is so.

Brendon and his lady-friend were connected and even met late to just touch one another. The lady wanted to give all she had to Brendon, yet Brendon was a bit afraid as this could easily lead to sin. So, he tried to talk to her, but she could not want to understand. This made her think that he does not like her. So, she was hurt by this. She even started losing weight. To Brendon's maturing mind from that trauma, this all seemed like a dream. Even when he loved her, he still asked himself how and why he accepted her in his life. In his brain, he remembered the trap.

"The way you wear determines the person inside you. For when you are about to clothe yourself, you think first. The one taking the decision to wear a mini skirt or a trouser is the one inside you. To prove this to you, have you ever seen a prostitute in suits? No, then that is not a prostitute because she will not attract men and get money.

Suits are not inside the prostitute. By the clothing you know their heart and inner man. But you know that sometimes the brain decides, where you see a farmer in a suit. But if you want to catch a person directly, check them when not going anywhere. You shall see the type of clothing one chooses automatically with the help of the one inside you. Beware of clothing, for it determines who you are to a stranger. If now I appear wearing dirty clothes, you might think I smoke nyaope, but if I appear in suits, you even respect me.

No one wants to step on a shoe of one wearing suits, for respect purposes induced by the type of clothing, but anyone can step on a tekkie and say I am sorry after. Amen" This is recorded by Brendon on one of the social media networks and sent it to all his connections. As they say a chicken flies with chickens not with eagles, that is if chicken fly.

So, you my friend, as I write to you about Brendon, don't you like someone like him? Don't you love him? Go to him and tell him how you feel about him. That is just some advice, because he has a list of girls to consider first before approaching another girl. Hence, represent yourself than never. Be strong like

Lindokuhle; She is a courageous young woman, Short, and a bit light and still dark. A curvy lady with so uniquely small nose and lips.

She is living her dream in real life because she stood up and fulfilled her dream. Therefore, you too buddy, do not burn in desire and do nothing. I do not promote girls approaching men, I am just introducing it further. Tell me, is there anything wrong there? I will approach if I am a woman, and I would accept if I were a man. It is life, we live according to our day light dreams which we put to action, no matter what.

I sometimes hate saying this, but nowadays girls are favourable than males. Check, for example, there is no sport that girls do not play, but you never see boys gathered playing net ball. So, this is very bad, because women said they want 50-50, but to be honest, according to my observation, they have more than 50%.

If you are a lady reading now, I am not against you, I am just stating facts. A certain writer named

Brendon once said; girls are like parasites, and boys are preys. This is true when checking life today. When something is tough, girls want a boy to go first, they say be a gentleman, then when something is very interesting, girls want to go first, they say girls first. Why do they put men to trouble always? Is it the mentality or the way they were raised?

Enough about that now, but I still have a bit to say; At why what we call love is not actually love. As I learned few things from Brendon when he preached, I learned that Love is God. So now if I ask what is love, people will be talking about pain. That is not love, it is dating, I think. We tend to use certain words where they are not needed. And that is vanity.

Chapter 4:

So now Brendon and his lady-friend live happy, they see each other more often than before. But as to all there is a bit of friction to strengthen whatever that is. Even to these two, a friction occurred, and now this friction was crucial. That if it occurs not, Brendon might not enjoy life in the future. It was exam time. All procedure was followed of registering for final exam, and all necessary stuff.

This exam period was very important to Brendon that he remembered all words from his mother about grade 12, that once you share your focus between books and any other thing accept prayer, because prayer is like breathing, you cannot live without it. So, Brendon said he must now focus on exams 100%.

He had to either stop the relationship or just give it a break. "I think we should give it a break." Brendon said. "Why? Are you seeing another person?" The girl said. "No, not now. I am about to write my final exams, which will never occur again. So, I need to study harder and not sleep, that in the future will work easy and sleep." Brendon adds. "Why? Do I disturb you...But I understand, go ahead!".

"Thanks for understanding. One more thing, I will delete this app (Social media app), because every second I waste starring at it, I should be revising what I did since I was introduced to schooling." Brendon said. "Ok, go ahead! But in will miss you." The lady said. "Do not worry, by God's Grace, I will see you after these exams. I will miss you too, but I need to forget about you during these upcoming exams. Hope you are fine." "Yes, I am fine". "Ok, this is a goodbye for a while." "Ok, sure."

These two spoke and spoke about future on how to prepare better for the it, I want to be like this guy. I cannot wait to ask Brendon how to come he is like this. Brendon, I see, he is very different, even those who hate him, it is not because of his bad behaviour, it is because they are jealous. But to tell you something, most who hate his parents hate him also, and some hate him, not his behaviour or his parent. This all is how life is, your never liked by everyone. Never!

They remind me of Romeo and Juliet, these are my Romeo and Juliet. It came to pass that Brendon cut off all connections in social media, then he focused on exams. His timetable was quite unfair before him, because it had all tough papers adjacent to each other, with only one or two days to prepare for one tough paper, yet about five to eleven days to prepare for easy papers which needs not to be prepared.

This even before my eyes was unfair, but every bad thing, has a positive side to see. Just as one wise man said, in the mist of dark clouds, you can be able to see a little star. Beloved! Love is blind as they say, but to be honest, it is new love which takes you to an unconscious state, that you see thing yet not perceive. How bad is that?

But to this there is a little star, that when your unconscious, you can be able to focus on one thing and be able to excel at it.

Brendon wrote his first paper, English paper 1. It was just easy for him, but that doubt which always attacks learners that you think maybe there is a mistake you did without seeing. What I like about what Brendon did is that he did his promise, that he should forget about any other thing. Just to focus only on books, preparing like his life depends on the score he will get on that paper. He writes Accounting just few days from his first paper.

He wrote Maths's paper 1 a day after accounting paper. When he was to write Maths's paper 2, he then started developing stress, because he did not finish writing Accounting, and he only left about 5 marks in Paper 1. He needed to excel in paper 2, which he struggled on, because if he performs bad, his results would be messed up. You see, it is somehow, that if someone scores around 40%

usually, when he scores 50%, he will celebrate as the teacher that marks would say 'very good' or 'keep it up'.

Then when him who scores 80s every time, if scores 79%, he will be feeling very bad, that even the teacher who marks the paper will write 'very bad' at the cover. He will not be grateful that he managed to score most and missed less. Even Brendon was like that, if he misses one question, he says the paper was so tough. That is how different people of different capabilities are.

Brendon had to try hard to clear all that stress of not finishing other papers, because he knew that once he is stressed from ne paper, that can easily affect other papers. He loved being on one paper and thinking only about it when about to write it. For every subject is a planet on its own.

This is vanity, as said by the wisest man in Jerusalem ever (King Solomon, the son of King David). This I also learned from Brendon. I hope since you started reading, you learned something about Brendon, and love something. Or are you like his enemies, which he loves? Whom hate him for doing good?

He wrote his fourth paper, then another until his last paper. He was really working, that if he usually performs bad on a paper, he did not sleep the whole night before the final paper, preparing for it. In the morning taking a cold bath and going into the exam room. I remember one mistake he did, yet by GOD's Grace he managed to write well, when he was preparing for Life Sciences paper 2, he did not sleep the whole night, then in the morning, instead of taking a cold bath, he took a warm one.

After arriving at the exam room one hour before the commencement of the exam, he slept, yet woke up when people were checking the paper, about to write. He remembered all he did though. That means there is something mysterious about a cold bath.

After taking a cold bath, he does not sleep at all the whole day until he will sleep at 7 later.

Brendon has several meanings, one of them is a mountain covered with prolific weed, somewhere there. Check it! Even your name if you know not what your name stands for. Enough about this! Brendon was done with his exams now, then he had to reconnect.

No one could send him the things he deleted, so the lady realised that Brendon is done, yet not coming back from break, so she thought this was over. She was really hurt because she did not want Brendon to leave her. She knew that there are many looking for Brendon specifically, the entire school. She was very scared of losing him so soon.

Since when they meet, they talk on the social media first about what time they are to meet, so now there was no connection between them for about two weeks after exams. Lindokuhle even lost few kilograms of lipids. Brendon was too rich to buy airtime, he could not afford it, since he needed money for many things around him.

Yet Lindokuhle managed to buy some, sacrificing for the thing she has for that young man, and called Brendon, but mostly Brendon was too busy and only found missed calls. This even made Lindokuhle feel extremely bad about her love. She did not know Brendon's home that she might go and see him, so she concluded that Brendon cut off ties. But one time she manages get Brendon. "Hey! How are you doing lady?" Brendon answers the phone. "How are you treating me? You're hurting me do you know that?", the lady says. "How so? What have I done?"

"Ok, just forget it". "Ok then but know that I am about to install that app, I really need it. Can we meet at school tomorrow that you send it to me, so we can connect again?" Brendon asks. "I don't think so; I will see tomorrow." "So, let it be, maybe I will manage to get it though." "Bye!" "Bye!".

Chapter 5:

Exams are over, and the only thing crucial Brendon is waiting for, are the results. He is now connected back to Lindokuhle. "Can I ask you a silly question?" Lindokuhle asks on the social media app. Then Brendon takes time to respond, as he is still sucking his cerebrum (Portion of the brain, responsible for higher thoughts).

"I am just asking, I am not going to ask a stupid question, just a silly one." Lindokuhle adds. "Ok, go ahead then." Brendon approves. "What would you do if I am pregnant?" Lindokuhle asks. "Not that I am pregnant". She adds. The Brendon in his heart say: Actually, I was living a good life before I dated, this brings more pain and sorrow to me. It seems good outside, yet inside it is bitter.

"I would only ask you three questions; 1. Who is responsible for that. 2. What do you want me to do. 3. Did you cheat? And do you want me to leave?" Brendon answers her with questions. "Mm! You are different from others. And I love you for that variance." Lindokuhle says. "How so?" "No, just. You are so different that your difference is so good.

I have been waiting for this type of a person for a long time. As my name says (Lindokuhle-Wait for the better)." Lindokuhle said. "Ok…". The two were good now, and their relationship was known before many.

People start talking about this matter even on the streets. Some are even courageous enough to come and confront Brendon the young preacher. His answers are like rhetoric questions. He answered one of them saying; "Good or bad you do, people will talk. It is good to talk, but too much of that becomes pathogenic.

Check, in the Bible, people were able to know that Jesus Christ is approaching their country. How was it done? Were they prophets? No. It is because of those who speak. Speaking about what you observe to others is good yet living most of your life seeking people's matters, so you can discuss them, you will not get paid. You are just wasting more time than sleeping. Even I, do speak about people, but only what is profitable to listeners. Even you, make sure when you speak about me to others, you speak what will profit their lives when they hear it."

Brendon said these words directly not whispering, that even the surrounding ears heard it clearly. "To say I am dating I would be lying, because I don't understand the meaning of that. I am not an English; all I know is that I and Lindokuhle are knowing each other better." Brendon adds.

Brendon from that time lived most of his life being asked about his relationship with Lindokuhle. He answered all questions asked according to the way he thought was right. He spoke many confusing words, which listeners had to ask for clarity: "When one is given a plate full of food to eat, and a fork, he will eat that which is suitable for eating and leave the plate and the fork, no matter how hungry he can be.

Because the plate and the fork are not for eating."
Brendon said. "What do you mean by that Brendon".
They asked. "This is very simple; I mean that there
are many girls who wish to be with me, yet some are
like fork, not suitable for eating, just using them to
eat. I mean they are not good for me, I just leave
near them for life to seem like life, because without
them around me, life will not be life. In the Jungle,
lions would not eat plants but animals, and springbok
would not eat animals but plants."

Brendon adds. "Then by that what do you mean?"
They asked again. "I mean that not all girls in this
world, no matter how beautiful they might be, are for
people like me. Even some girl's dream men are
thieves. They have their own reasons for that, just
like those who have reasons for liking me. For I have
realised something in life, to everything, there are
always two sides, that is why you see two going to
court even when the matter is clear, just to please
the judge with their points.

This truly is vanity friends. There is only One True Judge, That Is Jesus Christ. Amen". Brendon always gave them hard stuff to solve, and sometimes even did not explain, to produce a negative catalyst to those coming to ask him questions. "To know if you good for singing, you heard people saying so when you sang, but sometimes some said you can't sing. You see that as people we are different?"

Brendon said. "So how do you connect this to our question?" They asked. "There is a variance between listening and hearing. And there is variance between seeing and perceiving. But this must happen, that one follows another, yet the other does not follow the other one. No man can marry unless it is arranged or have dated."

He spoke. "But I do not understand you Brendon". They spoke. "Even if I explain, some you will not understand, because I am not at the same level as you. And as most of you saying I am genetically mutated. Continue, for two blind men will talk most about what they hear, but not seeing even when they fall into a pit. Hahahaha, they will fall talking about what they heard, forgetting their ways.

"I am very sorry to say this, but I have no choice but to reveal it unto you; I hate Lindokuhle a lot, because she takes more of my feeling, she makes me feel different, and she took something which I once had unshared, and that is time. But to reveal it even more, I love her more than I hate her.

Then the conclusion of the matter is that I love her, even when I do not know what love is according to this world. I only know that Love is God, and if you Love God abides in you. I love her even when I do not understand this love they refer to as love not Love."

Then Brendon planned something which would make Lindokuhle smile a bit. He plans to write a short novel about that lady. He asks Lindokuhle about this and she happily agrees. Then Brendon begins that same night writing a book. He gives it a name and writes. He takes about two weeks writing and when he is done, he presents it as a free copy to the public. He also starts writing many books, like; She's Pretty, Spiritual, and many other.

He becomes an author even before the end of the year 2017. Then there are two big things he is waiting for then; Firstly, how Lindokuhle would react to the book he wrote, and secondly about his matric results. And that book which he wrote, it is this one you are reading.

He is still thinking about how Lindokuhle is going to react. Let us just hope the public and this lady would like it. It is titled 'Lindokuhle-The Advantageous Mutation'! For you to read, so you know a bit about what happened to me, and specially to Lindokuhle Dlamini.

THE END!

Purpose of this book:

This book is written to let people know about how different people are, and how they should react toward their differences. One should not agree to be changed by the environment, but rather change the environment, if you know you are right.

A friend once said; better be against time, than for time to be against you-Khotso 'Reigner' Ndowe. This is true, but for it to happen, you must first know yourself. The reason we seem very close to our parents but different from them is because of mutation.

But sometimes mutation is too much that we do not see the similarity, having white family but being black. So just know how mutated you are and act the way you are. You shall be against time. Another thing this book teaches, is that you must act on that which you wish to happen, do not easily break your life-plan promises.

For once you do that, your life is unplanned. Planning does not mean you will be that way, you need to act like Lindokuhle, and Julia did in this book, yet know that like Julia, sometimes things would not happen by plan. But other times like as to Lindokuhle, things will happen by your plan. If the thought scares you, wow, it is good to act upon.

The first step is to plan, work hard by actions, then manage your time. These three I was taught by Brendon when one day I asked him about how he succeeds. He said he makes a planning first, then work hard according to that planning, then lastly, he manages his time as he is working.

Title of the book:

It pleased the writer to write a short novel based on this title; Lindokuhle-Advantageous Mutation. The title and the story inside have a very close relationship, where Brendon, the main character had a certain behaviour which people thought he was genetically mutated.

This touch 'Mutation' on the title. Then he was uniquely wanted and loved for his behaviour, if indeed he was genetically mutated. This touch the 'Advantageous' part, as this type of difference Brendon had, was good. Then he had a relationship with a girl named Lindokuhle, just because of his good difference. Then all these combined to make up and come up with the title: Lindokuhle-Advantageous Mutation.

Words from the author:

This book, I wish that it be read in all the world, to bring motivation to those who are socially isolated, and who think they do not look and act like the rest of the group of people, and in turn, should thus do nothing to harm themselves just for fitting in. It is to all who support the talent of the author. Especially for some which I might name being Kamogelo, Khotso and all others who this book managed to reach them and read. I love you all guys. May God be with you all. **Luke 18 verse 27: Whatever impossible to men, with God it is possible.**

Cover:

The cover was created and sponsored by the Kindle Amazon team, as they are the ones who assisted in getting this book published.

Glossary:

In this book, the writer uses very simple English and a bit of science, the only names one can ask about are:

Crush- simply means a person you desire to be with, a person you like, a person you strongly love.
Mutated- to change or to develop in a different way
Vanity- too much pride in your appearance or achievements/ something which seems good, yet unprofitable, or leading to a non-good thing.
Variation- a difference.

This is a book to be read by all who can be able to read, regardless of age, race, geographical area. Being the first to be published by Brendon Mokalapa, more are coming, and many Thanks to the Almighty for granting the time, and all who played a part in it. Teachers, friends and loved ones.

www.ingramcontent.com/pod-product-compliance
Lightning Source LLC
Chambersburg PA
CBHW020330290526
45785CB00007B/2998